40 DAYS TO

Forever

Devotional Journey: Encountering God and Growing in His Word

Karyn Lee

Ark House Press
arkhousepress.com

Cataloguing in Publication Data:
Title: 40 Days to Forever
ISBN: 978-1-7637720-6-9 (pbk)
Subjects: REL012020, RELIGION / Christian Living / Devotional; REL012120, RELIGION / Christian Living / Spiritual Growth; REL034030, RELIGION / Holidays / Easter & Lent.

Design by initiateagency.com

DEDICATION

First, I would like to dedicate this book to God, our ABBA Father
Who invites us all into a relationship that is rich and fulfilling, I dedicate this devotional. May Your light guide us through these 40 days and beyond, illuminating our hearts and minds as we seek to grow in faith, love, and understanding

To those seeking a deeper connection with God,
This 40-day devotional journey is dedicated to the seekers, the questioners, and the believers. May these pages serve as a humble guide on your journey, providing moments of reflection, inspiration, and growth. As you turn each page, may you encounter the living Christ and be transformed by His Word.

To anyone who has ever felt distant or unsure,
May you find comfort in His presence and strength in His promises. This journey is for you—may it draw you closer to the heart of God and lead you to a deeper understanding of His boundless love.

Remember He is a Way maker, miracle worker, promise keeper
Light in the darkness, my God That is who He is

Song: *Way Maker*
Artist: Leeland Album: Better Word CCLI # 7115744 Lyrics:

You are here, moving in our midst
I worship You, I worship You
You are here, working in this place
I worship You I worship You
You are Way maker, miracle worker, promise keeper,
Light in the darkness, my God That is who You are

You are Way maker, miracle worker, promise keeper
Light in the darkness, my God That is who You are
You are here, touching every heart
I worship You I worship You
You are here, healing every heart
I worship You I worship You
You are here, turning lives around
I worship You I worship You
You are here, mending every heart
I worship You I worship You
That is who You are That is who You are That is who You are
That is who You are
Even when I don't see it, You're working
Even when I don't feel it, You're working
You never stop, You never stop working
You never stop, You never stop working

Amen.

Contents

Introduction

Welcome to this 40-day devotional journey
designed to help you encounter God and deepen
your relationship with God our Abba Father.

Each day, we will explore a different topic and provide
reflections, prayers, and Bible verses to guide you.
May this journey strengthen your faith and empower
you to grow in your relationship with God.

Let's begin!

DAY 1
EMBRACING GOD'S
PROFOUND LOVE

Reflect on the depth of God's love for you
Read John 3, focusing on verses 16-17

Deeper understanding and experience of God's love are our focus point today, take a moment to contemplate the boundless depth of God's love for us. It's a love beyond comprehension, limitless, and unconditional. God's incredible act of sacrifice, as described in "For God so loved the world that he gave his one and only Son, that whoever believes in him shall not perish but have eternal life...." - John 3:16–17

Pause for a moment; this love is beyond our understanding. Open your heart as you reflect on this verse.

Today, choose to embrace God's love. Let it transform your life, filling you with joy and peace. Make His love the cornerstone of your faith and relationship with Him.

In times of difficulty or uncertainty, remember that God's love is a constant wellspring of strength. Trust in His love, knowing that He is always with you, guiding you. Commit to seeking a deeper understanding and experience of God's love. May it overflow in your life, touching and transforming everything you do?

Prayer: *Heavenly Father, we thank You for Your incredible love. Help us grasp its depth and fully embrace it in our lives. Grant us a deeper understanding and experience of Your love. Fill us with Your love, so it overflows in our relationships, thoughts, and actions. Guide us on this journey of faith, enabling us to walk in Your love every day. In Jesus' name, Amen.*

DAY 2
SURRENDERING TO
GOD'S DIVINE PLAN

Explore the importance of surrendering to God's plans
Read Matthew 26, focusing on verse 39

Reflect on areas of your life where you need to surrender to God Jesus demonstrates a profound act of relinquishment in the Garden of Gethsemane as an inspiring illustration of God's divine plans for our lives. "Going a little farther, he fell with his face to the ground and prayed, 'My Father, if it is possible, may this cup be taken from me. Yet not as I will, but as you will.'" - Matthew 26:39

In this moment, Jesus, though human, surrendered His desires and fears to God's will. He trusted in God's perfect wisdom and love, understanding that divine plans exceed human comprehension. Consider your life. Are there dreams, ambitions, or tightly held plans you need to surrender to God? Release control and invite God's guidance. Surrendering isn't passive; it's an act of faith and trust, embracing God's extraordinary plan. It frees you from the burden of control, allowing God to lead you. As you embark on this surrender journey, pray for a willing heart to align with God's will. Ask Him to reveal resistance within, seek His guidance for decisions, and ask for His strength to let go.

Prayer: *Heavenly Father, today I surrender my life to Your will. Help me release my desires and trust in Your perfect timing and wisdom. Reveal areas of resistance and grant me strength to embrace Your plans. May I walk in obedience and faith, knowing Your ways are higher.*

In Jesus' name, Amen.

DAY 3
SEEKING GOD'S PRESENCE DAILY

Discover the significance of seeking God's presence in your daily life
Read Psalm 105, focusing on verse 4

Set aside dedicated time to seek God's presence today, let's explore the significance of seeking God's presence in our daily lives, guided by

"Look to the Lord and his strength; seek his face always." - Psalm 105:4

This verse encourages us to consistently seek God's presence, not just in times of need but in every aspect of life. Seeking God opens us to His strength, wisdom, and guidance.

Reflect on your life. Are there times you've neglected seeking God's presence, relying on your own strength? Let's commit to wholeheartedly seeking Him.

Dedicated time for seeking God's presence is essential. Whether through prayer, meditation, or reading His Word, prioritise this time to align with His will. In His presence, find peace and refuge. Know you're not alone in struggles; God guides every step. Seek Him to transform your perspective, shifting focus from worldly concerns to eternal truths. His wisdom reveals His plans. Seeking God's presence empowers you to reflect His love and grace. Be a vessel of His character and share His love. Commit to daily seeking God's presence. Prioritise this time to commune with Him, surrender to His will, and experience His transformative power. Let His love motivate you to impact others.

Prayer: *Heavenly Father, I seek Your presence daily. Help me prioritise this Time, free from distractions. Fill me with strength, wisdom, and guidance. Transform my perspective and use me to share Your love and grace. In Jesus' Name, Amen.*

DAY 4
GROWING IN FAITH

Learn about the process of growing in faith
Read Hebrews 11, focusing on verse 6
Reflect on ways you can actively grow in your faith

Nurturing Your Faith: Pleasing God, as it says in Hebrews 11:6, high-lights the crucial role of faith in our relationship with God. "Without faith, it is impossible to please God, because any-one who comes to him must believe that he exists and that he rewards those who earnestly seek him." - Hebrews 11:6

Stating that without it, pleasing God is impossible, as it requires belief in His existence and promises. Let's explore ways to actively nurture our faith. Faith is dynamic, requiring continuous care and attention. One way to grow in faith is by immersing ourselves in God's Word. The Bible provides wisdom, guidance, and promises. By engaging with Scripture daily, we deepen our understanding of God's character and His purpose for us. Regular Bible reading and meditation transform our minds and strengthen our faith.

Prayer is another avenue for faith growth. It's not just about making requests; it's a means of connecting with God, seeking His will, and aligning our hearts with His. Dedicate daily time to pray, both in joy and adversity. Purposeful prayer invites God into our lives, reinforcing our faith.

Build a community of fellow believers. Fellowship with like-minded individuals offers support, encouragement, and accountability. Engage in worship, join a small group, or seek mentors for your faith journey. Together, you can nurture your faith and inspire one another toward deeper intimacy with God. Embrace opportunities to step out in faith and trust God in new ways.

Often, faith flourishes during challenges and beyond our comfort zones. Trust in God's provision, guidance, and empowerment as you obey His leading. Growing in faith is a journey. Doubt, questions, and struggles may arise, but turn to God and lean on Him in those moments. Trust in His faithfulness, knowing He rewards those earnestly seeking Him.

Prayer: *Heavenly Father, I desire to nurture my faith. Guide me to seek You actively through Scripture, prayer, and fellowship with fellow believers. Strengthen my faith and deepen my trust in You. Grant me the courage to step out in faith and embrace the opportunities You present. May my faith please You and bring glory to Your name. In Jesus' name, Amen.*

DAY 5
TRUSTING GOD'S TIMING

Reflect on the importance of trusting God's timing
Read Ecclesiastes 3, focusing on verse 1
Pray for patience and trust in God's perfect timing

As we come to the 5th day, let's delve into a meaningful teaching of God's timing. In Ecclesiastes 3:1, have we not been reminded time and again that there's a season and a time for everything:

"To everything there is a season and a time for every purpose under heaven" - Ecclesiastes 3:1

This verse emphasizes that God is the master of time, with a perfect plan for each season in our lives. Trusting His timing brings us peace, contentment, and fulfilment.

Reflect on your life—are there areas where trusting God's timing is a challenge? Do impatience or the desire for quicker outcomes trouble you?

Today, surrender those concerns to God and choose to trust His timing. Trusting God's timing involves patience, faith, and surrender. It acknowledges His higher ways and eternal perspective. Even when we can't fathom His reasons, we trust that He works all things for our good. In times of waiting and uncertainty, turn to prayer. Pray for patience and a deeper trust in His timing. Ask God to calm your anxious heart as you wait on Him.

Also, remember that God's timing often aligns with our growth and preparation. While waiting, He may refine us, strengthen our faith, or equip us for the future. Embrace the process, knowing God works within you during the wait. Trusting God's timing involves surrendering your desires and agenda. It's an act of humility, acknowledging His superior plans. By yielding your timeline to Him, you open yourself to His best, even if it differs from your vision. Today, choose to trust God's timing in all aspects of life. Surrender your desires, plans, and expectations. Pray for patience, faith, and deeper trust. Rest in the knowledge that God is working all things for your good, and His timing is always perfect.

Prayer: *Heavenly Father, I surrender my desires and expectations to You. Grant me the strength to trust Your timing, even when it's challenging. Increase my patience and faith as I wait on You. Fill me with peace, knowing You're working everything for my good. May I find contentment and fulfilment in trusting Your perfect timing. In Jesus' name, Amen.*

DAY 6
DEVELOPING A PRAYERFUL LIFE

Our prayer and relationship with God daily are called for...
1 Thessalonians 5, focus on verses 16-18

In 1 Thessalonians 5:16-18, Day 6, we are urged to have a powerful prayerful life, as it has positive impacts on our connections with God.

"Rejoice always, pray continually, and give thanks in all circumstances; for this is God's will for you in Christ Jesus...." - Thessalonians 5:16-18

These verses highlight a strong focus on our daily prayer lives. It transcends mere religious duty or seeking our needs; it's a means to commune with God, seek His guidance, and express gratitude. Through it, we align our hearts with Him and experience His transformative work.

Take a moment to ponder your prayer life. Are there moments when you neglect communication with God or relegate prayer to an afterthought? Today, let's commit to setting aside dedicated time for prayer. Allocate time today to pray and seek God's presence. Find a quiet space for intimate communion with Him. Pour out your heart, share your thoughts, and lay your burdens before Him. In prayer, we engage with our God, who listens and responds to our heartfelt cries.

Moreover, prayer fosters gratitude. When we thank God in all circumstances, we recognize His goodness, faithfulness, and provision. Even in adversity, we find reasons for gratitude, knowing God orchestrates all things for our benefit. Let gratitude accompany your prayer life, deepening trust and dependence on God. Developing a prayerful life entails maintaining an ongoing conversation with God throughout the day.

Pray continually, not just during designated times but in ordinary moments. Offer brief prayers of gratitude, guidance, and intercession as you go about your daily routines. This invites God into every facet of your life and acknowledges His presence in the mundane. As we commit to cultivating a prayerful life, remember that prayer isn't a one-sided dialogue. It's a relationship-building exercise with our Heavenly Father. Take time to listen to His voice, discern His will, and be open to His guidance. Be attentive to His communication through His Word, others, and the gentle whispers of His Spirit.

Prayer: *Heavenly Father, I yearn to nurture a prayerful life. Aid me in setting aside dedicated time for communion with You. Teach me to pray continuously, express gratitude in all circumstances, and attune my heart to Your voice. May my prayers deepen our relationship and impact the lives of others. In Jesus' name, Amen.*

DAY 7
UNDERSTANDING GOD'S WORD

**Reflect on the significance of studying
and understanding God's Word
Read Psalm 119, focusing on verse 105
Commit to reading and studying the Bible regularly**
"Your word is a lamp for my feet, a light on my path" - Psalm 119:105

Demonstrates the power of God's Word, providing illumination and guidance for our lives and inspiring us to consider our relationship with the Bible. Think for a moment to reflect on how to interact with the Bible. Have you been neglecting it? Let's commit to regular Bible study to gain a deeper understanding of God's truths.

Regularly reading and studying the Bible is vital for a strong faith foundation. Immersing ourselves in Scripture deepens our knowledge of God, His character, and His plans. Priorities daily dedicated time for reading and meditation to shape your thoughts and actions.

Furthermore, studying the Bible helps us discern truth from falsehood in a world of conflicting messages. It serves as an unchanging anchor, offering timeless wisdom to navigate life's complexities. Approach the Bible with humility and a teachable spirit, recognizing it as a living word from God. Invite the Holy Spirit to guide your study, reveal truths, and transform your heart and mind. Studying God's Word deepens our relationship with Him.

It's through scripture that we encounter the living God, drawing closer and experiencing His love, grace, and presence. Exploring God's Word reveals our identity and purpose. It reveals God's love, His redemptive plan, and our worth as His beloved children. This empowers us to live out our calling confidently and purposefully. Today, commit to studying and understanding God's Word. Set aside daily time for reading and meditation. Approach it with an open heart to encounter God and gain wisdom, guidance, and a deeper understanding of yourself in Him.

Prayer: *Heavenly Father, I commit to studying and understanding Your Word. Help me dedicate daily time to Scripture. Open my heart and mind to receive Your truths and be transformed by Your Word. Guide me through Your Spirit, deepening my relationship with You as I seek to understand Your Word. In Jesus' name, Amen.*

DAY 8
EXPERIENCING GOD'S
FORGIVENESS

**Contemplate the profound depth of God's forgiveness
and the essential act of forgiving others.
Read Matthew 6, focusing on verses 14-15
Focus and seek a heart open to forgiveness.**

In today's reflection on the transformative power of forgiveness, Matthew 6:14-15 underscores its pivotal role in our connection with God: "If you forgive others when they wrong you, your heavenly Father will also forgive you. But if you refuse to forgive others, your Father will not forgive you."

These verses emphasise forgiveness's importance in our lives. Let's delve into the boundless and unconditional nature of God's forgiveness. Despite our sins, God's mercy is always accessible. Through Jesus Christ's sacrifice, God offers forgiveness, cleansing us from our sins and reconciling us with Him.

Consider the forgiveness you've received from God. Are there areas where accepting His forgiveness proves challenging? Open your heart to fully experience God's forgiveness, allowing it to revolutionise your life. Encountering God's forgiveness compels us to extend the same grace to others. While not always easy, it is crucial for our well-being and growth. Clinging to grudges burdens us and impedes our spiritual progress.

When forgiving others, remember that it doesn't excuse the wrongs done to us. Instead, it's a conscious decision to release anger, resentment, and bitterness—a step toward healing.

Prayer serves as a potent tool to nurture a forgiving heart. Pray for a heart willing to forgive, even when it seems impossible. Seek God's assistance in releasing past hurts, allowing His love and grace to fill you. Trust in His ability to restore and heal as you choose forgiveness. Forgiveness is an ongoing process, especially in cases of profound hurt or betrayal. Be patient with yourself and others on this journey. Lean on God's strength and seek support from trusted friends or mentors.

Prayer: *Heavenly Father, grant me Your forgiveness and enable me to embrace it wholly. Soften my heart to forgive others as You have forgiven me. May I be a vessel of Your love, extending forgiveness to all who have wronged me. In Jesus' name, I pray. Amen.*

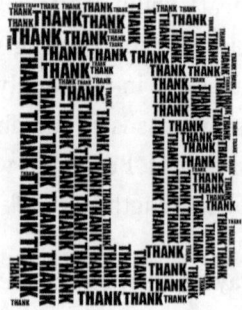

DAY 9
CULTIVATING A GRATEFUL
HEART: A JOURNEY OF FAITH

Discover the power of gratitude in your relationship with God
Read 1 Thessalonians 5, focusing on verse 18
Reflect on the blessings in your life and express gratitude to God

In our faith journey, nurturing a grateful heart is profoundly transformative. Gratitude draws us closer to God, enriches our relationship with Him, and positively impacts humanity. Let's explore its significance. "Give thanks in all circumstances; for this is God's will for you in Christ Jesus." - 1 Thessalonians 5:18

True gratitude thrives when we choose to be thankful, even amid challenges. Reflect on life's blessings, from shelter and food to love and relationships. Cultivating a grateful heart allows us to appreciate life's meaningful details.

Gratitude deepens our connection with God. It acknowledges His sovereignty and love, drawing us closer to Him. It fosters trust, love, and reverence in our relationship. Gratitude's impact extends beyond personal growth. It's contagious, making us more compassionate and considerate. This positivity enriches our interactions, bridging divides and fostering unity.

Imagine a world where everyone embraces gratitude, appreciates blessings, and acknowledges others' contributions. Such a world would overflow with love, empathy, and joy.

Prayer: *Heavenly Father, I'm grateful for life's blessings, big and small. Help me embrace gratitude in all circumstances. Teach me to appreciate others, be a source of love and kindness, and make a positive difference in the world. Amen.*

DAY 10
SPREADING GOD'S LOVE

Explore the significance of sharing God's love with others
Read Matthew 28, focusing on verses 19-20
Identify opportunities to show God's love to those around you

Today, we explore the profound theme of sharing God's love as we continue our faith journey. This mission is pivotal, impacting individual lives and shaping humanity. Matthew 28:19-20 echoes Jesus' commission to His disciples: "Go and make disciples of all nations...teaching them to obey everything I have commanded you."

This emphasizes actively sharing God's love and message, transcending boundaries. Sharing God's love involves proclaiming the Gospel and embodying Christ's love through our actions. Being compassionate, kind, and understanding is vital. We become living testimonies of God's grace and mercy. Opportunities to demonstrate God's love abound in our daily lives.

Listening to a friend in need, offering assistance, or providing encouragement can profoundly impact others, spreading hope and healing. Engaging in community service and supporting marginalized individuals are tangible ways to show God's love. Volunteering, aiding charitable organizations, or participating in outreach programs make a significant difference.

Sharing God's love also entails embracing diversity, treating all with respect and dignity, and fostering unity and harmony. Our love should mirror God's boundless love.

As we heed the call to share God's love, we become agents of transformation. Each act, no matter how small, has a ripple effect, touching countless lives. By living out the Great Commission, we contribute to a world where love, compassion, and understanding prevail, profoundly impacting Humanity.

Prayer: *Heavenly Father, guide me to be a vessel of Your love. Help me show kindness, compassion, and inclusivity. May my actions reflect Your love, bring hope, and contribute to spreading Your message of grace and salvation. Amen.*

DAY 11
CONQUERING FEAR AND ANXIETY

Reflect on God's promise to be with you and provide peace
Read Isaiah 41, focusing on verse 10
Pray for the strength to overcome fear and anxiety

In our faith journey, we often face fear and anxiety. However, we find reassurance and strength in God's promise to be with us and grant us peace amidst life's challenges. Isaiah 41:10 offers this comforting message. God assures us in "Do not fear, for I am with you; do not be dismayed, for I am your God. I will strengthen you, help you, and uphold you with my righteous right hand." - Isaiah 41:10

These words remind us that we're not alone; God provides strength and guidance. Fear and anxiety often stem from uncertainty about the future or life's challenges. Yet, we serve a God who holds the universe and cares deeply for us. He knows our struggles and promises unwavering love and protection. Through prayer, we seek strength to conquer fear and anxiety, pouring out our concerns to God. Surrendering these burdens opens us to His transcendent peace, guarding our hearts and minds in life's storms.

Prayer: *Heavenly Father, in moments of fear and anxiety, I turn to You. Thank You for Your promise to be with me and provide peace. Strengthen me with Your unwavering love and help me overcome my fears. I trust in Your righteous right hand to uphold me. Grant me the peace that surpasses all understanding as I surrender my worries to You. Amen.*

DAY 12
STRENGTHENING FAITH
THROUGH RELATIONSHIPS

Discover the importance of healthy
relationships in your faith journey
Read Proverbs 27, focusing on verse 17
Reflect on ways to strengthen your relationships with others

In our faith journey, our relationship with God takes precedence as the bedrock of spiritual growth. However, it's vital to acknowledge the profound influence of healthy human connections on our spiritual development. Our interactions with others should be like the sharpening of iron: "As iron sharpens iron, so one person sharpens another." Proverbs 27:17

Just as iron gains sharpness by rubbing against another, our character, faith, and understanding mature through meaningful interactions with fellow believers. Meaningful, healthy relationships offer companionship, accountability, and growth prospects. They enable us to encounter God's love, grace, and compassion through the individuals He places in our lives. By fostering positive relationships, we not only fortify our faith but also cultivate a supportive, uplifting environment for others.

Here are strategies to enrich your relationships:

1. Be intentional:
   a. Actively connect with others, showing genuine interest in their life journeys.
2. Practice active listening:
   a. Engage empathetically when others express their thoughts and feelings.
3. Extend Grace and Forgiveness:
   a. Promote an environment of reconciliation and growth by offering grace and forgiveness during challenges.
4. Serve One Another:
   a. Strengthen bonds through acts of kindness and Selflessness.
5. Pray for One Another:
   a. Unite hearts in prayer, inviting God's presence into your relationships.

By investing in fortifying these relationships, we contribute to a community that mirrors Christ's love. Our lives become testimonials of His transformative power, drawing others closer to Him through bonds of fellowship and love.

Prayer: *Heavenly Father, we thank you for the gift of relationships and their profound impact on our faith journey. Guide us in nurturing healthy, meaningful connections that sharpen and uplift one another in our walk with You. Endow us with wisdom, grace, and a servant's heart. May our relationships radiate Your love and glorify Your name. Amen.*

DAY 13
DISCOVERING UNSHAKABLE
HOPE IN CHRIST

Reflect on the hope that comes from your relationship with Jesus
Read Romans 15, focusing on verse 13

Pray for an unwavering hope in Christ during challenging times amid life's trials and uncertainties, our connection with Jesus serves as an Unswerving wellspring of hope. He anchors our souls, offering solace, fortitude, and assurance.

Let's ponder the hope that stems from our knowledge of Him and reflect on Romans 15:13 as a reminder of the abundant hope we possess in Christ.

Life's tribulations can leave us feeling overwhelmed, anxious, or uncertain about the future. In these moments, we can turn to Jesus, our unwavering hope. Our hope in Christ isn't tethered to transient circumstances but is rooted in His immutable character and promises. "May the God of hope fill you with all joy and peace as you trust in him so that you may overflow with hope by the power of the Holy Spirit." - Romans 15:13

This verse beautifully encapsulates the essence of hope in Christ. It underscores that God is the source of hope. As we entrust ourselves to Him, He infuses us with joy, peace, and overflowing hope through the Holy Spirit's work.

Our hope in Christ allows us to persevere with courage in the face of adversity, knowing He reigns. We find peace in His presence, strength in His Word, and certainty in His love. Our hope is anchored in His unchanging nature; He is the same yesterday, today and forever more. Through our hope in Christ, we become beacons of light and agents of hope for those around us. Our lives bear witness to the transformational power of faith, inspiring others to seek the hope only Jesus provides. As we radiate His hope, we uplift and encourage those enduring difficult times, pointing them toward the ultimate wellspring of enduring hope and serenity.

Prayer: *Heavenly Father, we thank you for the hope we uncover in Christ. During trying times, we seek You as our sanctuary and anchor. As we entrust ourselves to You, fill us with joy, peace, and overflowing hope through the Holy Spirit's power. Help us cling to this unshakeable hope in Christ, even when circumstances appear uncertain. May our lives testify to Your faithfulness and grace, impacting those around us with the hope found solely in You. Amen.*

DAY 14
THE PROFOUND IMPACT OF
HUMILITY IN OUR WALK WITH GOD

Explore the significance of humility in your relationship with God
Read Philippians 2, focusing on verses 3-4

Reflect on areas in your life where you can grow in humility. Humility is a profound virtue in our connection with God. It opens our hearts to His presence, recognizing His sovereignty and grace. Let's delve into the impact of humility on encountering God, reflect on Philippians 2:3-4, and explore areas where we can cultivate more humility. The trait of humility is completely different from pride, which can form obstacles between us and God. By having a humble approach towards God, we confess that we depend on Him and recognize that He is the root of all knowledge, power, and morality. This type of modest outlook permits us to accept God's affection and direction by giving up our self-sufficiency and preferring His wishes rather than our own.

Philippians 2:3-4 provides guidance

"Do nothing out of selfish ambition or vain conceit. Rather, in humility, value others above yourselves, not looking to your own interests but each of you to the interests of others."

This Scripture encourages us to focus on others with genuine care and empathy, setting aside selfish desires. When we practice humility in our interactions, we create an atmosphere of love, unity, and understanding. Take a moment to reflect on areas where you can nurture humility. This self-examination may reveal moments when pride creeps in, such as seeking recognition, making comparisons, or hesitating to serve those we consider less important. Identifying these areas allows us to actively cultivate a humble heart, aligning with Christ's example.

Encountering God with humility transforms us in His presence. Our hearts become receptive to His guidance, deepening our intimacy with our Heavenly Father. As we continue our faith journey, let's remember the significance of humility and its influence on our relationship with God and Humanity.

Prayer: *Heavenly Father, we thank you for Jesus' example of humility. Guide us as we grow in humility, recognizing our dependence on You and esteeming others above ourselves. Reveal areas where pride hinders our relationships with You and others. May our encounters with You be marked by humble hearts, open to Your wisdom and grace. Use us as vessels of Your love and compassion, impacting humanity to reflect Your character. Amen.*

DAY 15
EXPERIENCING GOD'S PRESENCE IN WORSHIP

Discover the role of worship in your relationship with God
Read Psalm 100, focusing on verse 2

Engage in meaningful worship today and express your love to God Worship holds a crucial role in our connection with God. It's a powerful means to draw near to Him, encounter His presence, and express our love and adoration. Let's explore the importance of worship and contemplate

Psalm 100:2 as we engage in meaningful worship today, offering our hearts and voices to God.

Worship isn't a mere ritual or routine; it's a heartfelt response to God's greatness and goodness.

Psalm 100:2 beautifully captures this essence:

"Worship the Lord with gladness; come before him with joyful songs." When we approach God with gladness and joy, raising our voices in praise, our hearts align with His, and we experience His presence in a profound way. In worship, we fix our attention on God, leaving behind distractions and worldly concerns. It's a time of surrender, where we release our burdens and find rest in His presence. Through worship, we acknowledge His sovereignty and worthiness, recognizing that He alone deserves our praise and Devotion.

Meaningful worship deepens our relationship with God. We open our hearts, allowing His love and grace to transform us from within.

Worship reminds us of His faithfulness and goodness, strengthening our faith and trust in Him.

The impact of worship goes beyond our individual encounters with God. When we join others in corporate worship, we become part of a community united in adoration. Our collective voices rise like a symphony of praise, reflecting the diversity and beauty of humanity's worship of its Creator. By expressing our love for God through worship, we influence the world around us. Our worship becomes a testament to God's love, drawing others to seek Him and encounter His presence. Through our worship, we inspire hope, provide healing, and share the message of God's grace with those who may not yet know Him.

So, let's engage in worship today with hearts full of gladness and joy. May our songs and prayers be offerings of love to the One who loves us immeasurably. In worship, may we encounter God's presence and be transformed by His unwavering love.

Prayer: *Heavenly Father, we thank you for the gift of worship, where we can draw near to You and experience Your presence. Today, we come before You with gladness and joy, lifting our voices in praise and adoration. As we worship You, may our hearts be transformed by Your love and grace. Use our worship to impact others, reflecting Your goodness and drawing them closer to You. Amen.*

DAY 16
EMBRACING SERVICE: UNCOVERING OPPORTUNITIES TO SERVE

Exploring Acts of Love and Service
Understanding the Significance of
Serving in Jesus' Name
Read Mark 10, focusing on verse 45

In our modern, fast-paced world, where self-interest often takes precedence, the act of serving others carries immense spiritual importance. Jesus, the epitome of love and compassion, exemplified the significance of selfless service during His earthly tenure. Let's delve into the profound message conveyed in Mark 10:45 and learn how we can embody Jesus' heart of service in our lives.

"For even the Son of Man did not come to be served, but to serve, and to give his life as a ransom for many." - Mark 10:45 this scripture encapsulates the core of Jesus' earthly mission. He didn't seek admiration or praise; instead, He humbly served others with boundless love and compassion. In our daily lives, this means actively seeking opportunities to assist and uplift others, not for personal recognition but to mirror the love of Christ.

Serving others in the name of Jesus is a tangible expression of our faith. It transcends mere assistance; it embodies Jesus' teachings through our actions. When we serve with love and compassion, we become channels of God's grace, reflecting His unconditional love for those around us. Through serving, we actively partake in God's divine plan, spreading kindness and instilling hope in a world often mired in despair.

Reflect upon the unique gifts and talents bestowed upon you by God. Ponder how these abilities can be utilized to serve others. It might entail volunteering at a local shelter, mentoring a struggling friend, supporting a charitable cause, or simply offering a listening ear to someone in need. Acts of service, regardless of their scale, possess the power to profoundly impact lives and glorify God.

Prayer: *Heavenly Father, We express gratitude for the exemplary life of Your Son, Jesus Christ, who came not to be served but to serve. Open our eyes to the people who need You. Strengthen our hearts, O Lord, and lead us in our endeavors to reflect Your love through our actions. May our service stand as a testimony to Your grace and bring honor to Your name. In Jesus' name, we pray. Amen.*

As we meditate on Mark 10:45, let's wholeheartedly embrace the call to serve others with love and compassion. Through our actions, we not only fulfil God's commandment but also reflect the heart of Jesus to a world thirsting for His love. Let our deeds serve as beacons of hope, illuminating every corner of our lives with the radiant light of Christ.

DAY 17
FINDING STRENGTH IN WEAKNESS

Reflect on God's power and strength in your moments of weakness
Read 2 Corinthians 12, focusing on verse 9

Pray for God's strength to be made perfect in our weakness today, let's ponder the significance of humility in finding strength during our weakest moments, recognizing that it's precisely in these times that we can witness the full extent of God's power and might. Often, our human nature pushes us to rely on our own abilities. However, when we acknowledge our vulnerabilities and yield to God, we discover genuine strength.

In 2 Corinthians 12:9, the apostle Paul shares a powerful insight: "But he said to me, 'My grace is sufficient for you, for my power is made perfect in weakness.' Therefore, I will boast all the more gladly about my weaknesses, so that Christ's power may rest on me."

These words emphasize that true victory doesn't stem from our own strength but from God's divine power working through us. When we humbly admit our limitations, we create space for God's strength to shine through our weaknesses. In those moments of surrender, we experience the grace and power of God at work within us. Our weaknesses don't limit God; rather, He seizes them as opportunities to showcase His power and glorify His name.

Take a moment to reflect on your own weaknesses and areas where you might feel inadequate. Instead of being disheartened by them, invite God into those very spaces. Ask Him to infuse you with His strength, surrendering your weaknesses to His care. Trust that His power will radiate brilliantly through your moments of weakness.

Prayer: *Dear Heavenly Father, We thank you for the profound reminder that Your grace is more than enough for us, and Your power is most fully realized in our weaknesses. Grant us the ability to embrace our vulnerabilities and place them in Your loving hands. Fill us with Your unwavering strength, enabling us to lean on You in every facet of our lives. May Your magnificent power shine through us, bringing honour to Your name. We pray this in Jesus' name. Amen.*

DAY 18
PURSUING HOLINESS

Reflect on the call to live a holy life for God
Read 1 Peter 1, focusing on verses 15-16

Identify areas in your life where you can pursue holiness Today, let us reflect on the impact of humility in pursuing holiness. As followers of Christ, we are called to live a life that is set apart for God and marked by righteousness and purity. Our pursuit of holiness is not something we do in our strength; it is a response to God's call and a surrender to His transforming work in our lives.

"But just as he who called you is holy, so be holy in all you do; for it is written: 'Be holy, because I am holy.'" - 1 Peter 1:15-16

These verses remind us that God, who is holy, has called us to reflect His holiness in everything we do. Pursuing holiness is not about earning our salvation; it is a response to the grace and love that God has shown us.

Humility plays a crucial role in our pursuit of holiness. It is through humility that we recognize our need for God's guidance and transformation in our lives. We acknowledge that we cannot achieve holiness on our own, but we depend on God's grace and the power of the Holy Spirit to work in us. Take a moment to reflect on your own life. In what areas can you pursue holiness? It may be in your thoughts, words, actions, or relationships. Ask God to reveal any areas where you need to grow in holiness and humility. Surrender those areas to Him and seek His guidance and strength to live a life that honours Him.

Prayer: *Dear Heavenly Father, thank You for calling us to a life of holiness. Help us to pursue holiness with humility, knowing that it is only through Your grace and power that we can grow in righteousness. Show us any areas in our lives where we need to grow in holiness and give us the strength to surrender those areas to You. May our pursuit of holiness bring glory to Your name and draw others closer to you. In Jesus' name, we pray. Amen.*

DAY 19
BUILDING A
CHRIST-CENTRED FAMILY

Explore the importance of nurturing a Christ-centred family
Read Joshua 24, focusing on verse 15

Pray for your family's faith to be strengthened and centred on Jesus Today, let's delve into the crucial significance of nurturing a Christ-centred family amidst the distractions and competing priorities of the world. In the words of Joshua 24:15, he powerfully declares to the Israelites: "But if serving the LORD seems undesirable to you, then choose for yourselves this day whom you will serve... But as for me and my household, we will serve the LORD." Joshua recognized the profound importance of guiding his family in the ways of the Lord, deliberately prioritising God in their lives. To build a Christ-centred family, it begins with our personal commitment to follow Jesus. As our faith deepens, we can impart this faith to our family through our words, actions, and attitudes. Within our homes, we can create an atmosphere characterised by love, grace, and forgiveness, mirroring Christ's nature.

Reflect on your family. How can you nurture a Christ-centred environment within it? It might involve setting aside time for family devotionals, praying together, attending church collectively, or engaging in faith discussions. Ponder how you can consciously prioritise Jesus in your family's daily life.

Prayer: *Heavenly Father, We are grateful for the gift of family. Strengthen our family's faith and guide us in building a Christ-centred home. May our words, actions, and attitudes echo Your love and grace. Lead us in* *creating an environment where faith in Jesus flourishes. Assist us in making intentional choices that place You at the centre of our family life. In Jesus' name, we pray. Amen.*

As you continue this journey of fostering a Christ-centred family, remember that it's a gradual process. Be patient and steadfast in your efforts, trusting that God will honour your endeavours.

DAY 20
SEEKING WISDOM FROM GOD

Reflect on the value of seeking God's wisdom in decision-making
Read James 1, focusing on verse 5

Seek God's wisdom in a specific decision you are facing In our faith journey, seeking God's wisdom in decision-making holds immense importance, especially during pivotal moments. This practice showcases our reliance on His guidance and reveals our humility before our all-knowing Creator. Let's delve into the profound significance of seeking God's wisdom and ponder James 1:5 as we seek His guidance in specific decisions.

James 1:5 reassures us with these words: "If any of you lacks wisdom, you should ask God, who gives generously to all without finding fault, and it will be given to you." This promise underscores God's eagerness to provide wisdom to those earnestly seeking Him. We turn to the ultimate source of wisdom and knowledge rather than merely depending on our constrained comprehension.

Asking God for wisdom is a sign of confidence, a recognition that He knows what's best for us even when we don't fully understand the effects of our choices. By giving Him control over our plans, we make ourselves more receptive to His heavenly guidance.

External influences, such as societal expectations or personal ambitions, often cloud our judgement in decision-making. Seeking God's wisdom helps us sift through these distractions, aligning our hearts with His will. His wisdom brings clarity and peace amid uncertainty. As you contemplate a specific decision, earnestly seek God's wisdom through prayer and His Word. Be receptive to His guidance, even if it leads you in a different direction. Trust that His plans always work for your ultimate good.

By seeking God's wisdom, we not only make wiser decisions but also positively impact those around us. Following His guidance transforms us into vessels of His wisdom and grace, illuminating the world with His light.

Prayer: *Almighty Father, I come before You humbly, seeking your wisdom in the decision ahead of me. I trust in Your guidance, knowing You understand what's best. As I seek Your wisdom through prayer and Your Word, reveal my path. Align my desires with Your will, giving me the courage to follow Your lead, even in challenging times. Thank You for Your generous provision of wisdom. May my choices bring glory to Your name and positively influence others. Amen.*

DAY 21
EXPERIENCING GOD'S PEACE

Discover the peace that surpasses all understanding through Christ
Read Philippians 4, focusing on verse 7
Pray for God's peace to fill your heart and mind today
Discovering a peace that defies understanding
is possible through Christ.

The peace mentioned in Philippians 4:7, is profound. It is expressed independently of our circumstances and springs from the faith and trust we have in our Heavenly Father.

"And the peace of God, which transcends all understanding, will guard your hearts and your minds in Christ Jesus." - Philippians 4:7

This verse emphasizes that God's peace surpasses anything the world can offer, providing deep tranquility and assurance even amid life's uncertainties. In the presence of God's peace, fear, anxiety, and worry dissipate. We find comfort in the understanding that our Heavenly Father is in control, crafting a perfect plan for our lives. This peace doesn't rely on our abilities or circumstances; it is grounded in the unchanging character of God. Encountering this divine peace transforms our approach to life. We learn to release our worries, trusting that God will turn everything around for our good. This peace acts as a shield, protecting our hearts and minds from being overwhelmed by the world's challenges and enabling us to confront each day with confidence and hope. In moments of distress, we can actively seek God's peace through prayer. By entrusting our concerns to Him, we invite His peace to flood our hearts and minds. Through prayer, we acknowledge our dependence on Him, resting our trust in His unwavering love and wisdom.

Prayer: *Heavenly Father, I pray for Your peace to fill my heart and mind today. In life's uncertainties, help me to trust in Your plan and provision. Shield me from fear and anxiety, and grant me the peace that transcends understanding. May Your peace reshape how I approach challenges and uncertainties. Thank You for being my wellspring of strength and peace. In Jesus' name, Amen.*

DAY 22
WALKING IN GOD'S LIGHT

Reflect on the call to walk in God's light and live a righteous life
Read 1 John 1, focusing on verse 7

Examine areas of your life where you can align with God's light reflecting on the call to walk in God's light and live a righteous life is Essential for followers of Christ. This means aligning our lives with God's truth and allowing His guidance to illuminate our path. Let's contemplate this call and meditate on 1 John 1:7, focusing on areas in our lives where we can align ourselves with His light.

1 John 1:7 emphasizes, "But if we walk in the light, as he is in the light, we have fellowship with one another, and the blood of Jesus, his Son, purifies us from all sin."

Walking in God's light deepens our fellowship with Him and fellow believers. This intimate communion allows the cleansing and transforming power of Jesus' blood to wash away our sins, setting us on a righteous path. Walking in God's light demands humility, surrendering our will to His and seeking His guidance in every aspect of our lives. It means acknowledging our need for His wisdom and strength to live righteously. This journey involves regular self-examination, allowing God's light to reveal any hidden darkness or sin requiring His forgiveness and healing.

Consider areas in your life where alignment with God's light is necessary. Are there behavioral patterns or attitudes that need surrendering? Is there a need for forgiveness, either seeking it or extending it to others? Invite the Holy Spirit to reveal areas needing realignment with God's truth. As we walk in God's light and live righteously, our actions influence those around us. Our humility and obedience serve as a testament to God's transformative work, inspiring others to seek His light. Through our words and deeds, we can bring hope and encouragement, guiding others toward the true source of light and life—Jesus Christ.

Prayer: *Heavenly Father, thank you for calling us to walk in Your light and live righteously. As I examine my heart and actions, I reveal areas needing realignment with Your truth and forgiveness. Grant me the humility to surrender my will to yours and seek Your guidance in all I do. May my life testify to Your transforming power, offering hope and encouragement to others. In Jesus Name, Amen.*

DAY 23
GROWING IN PATIENCE

Explore the significance of patience in your faith journey
Read Romans 12, focusing on verse 12

Pray for patience in waiting on God's timing and plans Let's delve into the vital role of patience in our faith journey. Patience isn't merely a virtue; it's a fundamental quality as we navigate life's trials. Through patience, we learn to place our trust in God's timing and divine plans, even when uncertainty and anxiety cast shadows over us.

Romans 12:12 provides our guiding light: "Be joyful in hope, patient in affliction, and faithful in prayer."

These words emphasize the significance of patience in our connection with God. Patience equips us to endure challenging seasons, firmly believing that God is at work, even when the outcome remains unclear. It's through patience that our faith undergoes testing and refinement, and we draw closer to God. Patience isn't synonymous with passive waiting; it demands active trust in God's timing and intricate plans. It necessitates surrendering our desires and aligning ourselves with His flawless will. Patience nurtures perseverance, resilience, and a profound reliance on God.

Take a moment to ponder your own faith journey. Where do you need to cultivate patience? Are there situations where waiting on God's timing feels daunting? Surrender those areas to God and seek His guidance in developing patience and trust.

Prayer: *Heavenly Father, bestow upon us the gift of patience as we walk this journey with You. Grant us the ability to trust Your timing and plans, especially in moments of anxiety and uncertainty. Teach us to find joy in hope, to endure patiently in adversity, and to remain steadfast in prayer. Strengthen us when we struggle to wait on Your timing. May our lives bear witness to the patience and trust we place in You, bringing glory to Your name. In Jesus' name, we pray. Amen.*

Throughout your day, remember to nurture patience in all aspects of life. Trust in God's timing and plans, knowing that He is faithful and will unfailingly fulfill His promises. Let your patience serve as a testament to your unwavering faith in Him.

DAY 24
LOVING YOUR NEIGHBOUR

Reflect on the commandment to love your neighbour as yourself
Read Matthew 22, focusing on verse 39

Identify practical ways to demonstrate love to your neighbours today, let's delve into the profound directive of loving our neighbors as we love ourselves. In a world often marked by division and strife, it has become crucial for us to embody Christ's love and generously extend it to those around us. Jesus doesn't simply encourage us to speak of love; He challenges us to manifest it through tangible actions.

"You shall love your neighbour as yourself." - Matthew 22:39

The verse we're focusing on, Matthew 22:39, underscores the significance of treating others with love, kindness, and respect. Matthew is effectively teaching us how to interact with our fellow human beings, acknowledging their intrinsic worth as bearers of God's image. As we ponder this divine guidance, let's actively brainstorm practical ways to demonstrate love for our neighbours. It could be as simple as extending a helping hand, lending a compassionate ear, or infusing kindness into our everyday interactions.

Take a moment to consider whether there are specific individuals or communities you can support and uplift. Through prayer, seek guidance to identify tangible ways to exhibit God's love. Empower yourself to engage in acts of service and compassion.

Throughout your day, keep in mind the paramount importance of loving your neighbours. Actively seek opportunities to extend love, compassion, and unwavering support to those in your immediate vicinity. Let our actions speak louder than words; let Christ's love shine through our actions; and bring forth hope and healing to the desperate.

Prayer: *Heavenly Father, we stand before You in humility and adoration, thanking You for the crucial command to love our neighbours as ourselves. Grant us the strength to manifest this love through our actions. Illuminate practical ways for us to exhibit love to those around us. Open our hearts to perceive the needs of others and infuse in us the courage to respond with unwavering compassion and kindness. May our love mirror Yours and bring immense glory to Your holy name. In Jesus' name, we pray. Amen.*

DAY 25
TRUSTING GOD IN
TIMES OF TRIALS

Discover the faithfulness of God in times of trials and difficulties
Read Psalm 46, focusing on verses 1-2

Pray for trust and reliance on God in the midst of challenges in our life journey, we encounter a multitude of trials and tribulations, spanning in all directions, from financial hardship to health complications to difficulties in our relationships. You may say adversity is an inherent part of experience, knocking at different stages of our lives. In these very trying moments, we must maintain constant focus and cling to the unwavering belief that God is perpetually on our side, on which we can depend. Let us direct our focus to Psalm 46:1-2 and allow the profound truth within these verses to resonate deeply within our hearts:

"God is our refuge and strength, an ever-present help in trouble. Therefore, we will not fear, though the earth give way and the mountains fall into the heart of the sea."

These words stand as a poignant reminder that even when our world appears to crumble, God remains our sanctuary and the wellspring of our strength. His perpetual assistance serves as a guiding light, leading us through the trials we encounter. By entrusting our faith in Him, we can confront life's uncertainties without succumbing to fear. Let us take a moment to offer a heartfelt prayer, seeking profound trust and reliance on God amidst our challenges.

Prayer: *Heavenly Father, we humbly come before You with gratitude for being our refuge and strength during times of trial. We place our complete* *trust in You, acknowledging that our lives rest securely in Your hands. Strengthen us, O Lord, to confront challenges with unwavering confidence, always mindful of Your unwavering faithfulness. Grant us the wisdom to discern Your will and the grace to surrender our plans to You. We depend wholeheartedly on Your enduring love to carry us through. In the name of Jesus, we fervently pray. Amen.*

DAY 26
RECEIVING GOD'S GRACE

Reflect on the abundant grace that God freely offers
Read Ephesians 2, focusing on verses 8-9

Meditate on the significance of God's grace in your life let's delve into the profound gift of God's grace, a gift freely given to us despite our flaws and imperfections. Through His grace, we discover salvation and nurture a life-giving relationship with Him. Consider the magnitude of God's grace for a moment, and then read Ephesians 2:8-9 to fully grasp its significance.

Ephesians 2:8-9 reminds us, "For it is by grace you have been saved, through faith—and this is not from yourselves; it is the gift of God—not by works, so that no one can boast."

This verse emphasizes that our redemption is the consequence of God's unearned favour and kindness, not our own efforts. It underlines His boundless love and mercy, diving into our brokenness and giving forgiveness and new life in Christ.

As we contemplate the profound significance of God's grace, let's humbly acknowledge our need for it. Embracing the truth that His grace is freely given to all who believe in and receive Jesus Christ as their Savior, we recognize that we cannot save ourselves; our righteousness comes solely through Christ. God's grace profoundly impacts us, bringing transformation and liberating us from the chains of sin, empowering us to live a life that honors Him.

In receiving His grace, we are called to extend grace to others, demonstrating His love and compassion to a world in need.

Prayer: *Heavenly Father, we are profoundly grateful for Your abundant grace that saves and liberates us. We humbly receive this precious gift, fully aware that we cannot earn it. Help us grasp the immense significance of Your grace in our lives, bringing transformation and shaping us to resemble Jesus. As we ask in Your grace, empower us to extend the same love and compassion to others, impacting humanity and sharing Your salvation. In Jesus Name, Amen.*

DAY 27
PURSUING UNITY IN THE
BODY OF CHRIST

**Explore the importance of unity among believers in the Church
Read Romans 12, focusing on verses 4-5**

Reflect on ways you can contribute to unity in your church community today, let's explore seeking unity in the body of Christ. According to Paul in Romans 12:4-5, the body of Christ is made up of many parts, but all form one body. Unity among believers is essential for the church to function effectively. Just as a body needs all its parts working together, the church needs diverse individuals with unique gifts and roles, held together by unity. To contribute to unity in our church communities, we must value the uniqueness of each member. We should seek to understand and appreciate different gifts, perspectives, and experiences. Prioritizing others above ourselves and practicing humility and love builds connections and eliminates divisions. Healthy relationships, forgiveness, and reconciliation are crucial for nurturing unity.

Prayer plays a vital role in uniting believers. As we pray for one another, our hearts align with the Lord's desire for unity. Prayer allows us to set aside personal agendas and invite the Holy Spirit to guide and shape us into a united body.

In conclusion, pursuing unity in the body of Christ requires intentional effort. Let's remember that unity is a reflection of God's desire for His church. Together, let's actively work towards unity, embodying the love and grace of Christ that binds us together.

Prayer: *Heavenly Father, we acknowledge the significance of unity in the body of Christ. Help us embrace the uniqueness of each member, creating bridges of love and understanding. Guide us in practicing humility and selflessness. Pour out Your Spirit upon us, enabling us to put aside differences, forgive, and seek reconciliation. We thank You for the privilege of being part of Your church, and we pray for the manifestation of unity that brings glory to Your name. Amen.*

DAY 28
SHARING YOUR FAITH
WITH BOLDNESS

Reflect on the call to share your faith with confidence and boldness
Read Acts 4, focusing on verse 31

Pray for opportunities and courage to share your faith today, let's delve into the concept of fostering unity within the body of Christ. According to Paul in Romans 12:4-5, the body of Christ comprises diverse parts, yet they all form one cohesive unit. Unity among believers is essential for the church to function effectively. Just as a body relies on all its parts working harmoniously, the church thrives on diverse individuals with unique gifts and roles, bound together by the thread of unity. To promote unity in our church communities, it's crucial to value the distinctiveness of each member. Understanding and appreciating different gifts, perspectives, and experiences are vital. Prioritizing others over ourselves, practicing humility, and nurturing love build connections and dissolve divisive boundaries. Healthy relationships, forgiveness, and reconciliation are pivotal for nurturing and sustaining unity.

Prayer plays a vital role in uniting believers. When we pray for one another, our hearts align with the Lord's desire for unity. Prayer helps us set aside personal agendas, inviting the Holy Spirit to guide and mold us into a unified body. In conclusion, achieving unity in the body of Christ demands intentional effort. Let's always keep in mind that unity mirrors God's desire for His church. Together, let's actively strive for unity, embodying the love and grace of Christ that bind us together.

Prayer: *Heavenly Father, we acknowledge the paramount importance of unity within the body of Christ. Help us embrace the uniqueness of each member, building bridges of love and understanding. Guide us in practicing humility and selflessness. Pour out Your Spirit upon us, enabling us to set aside differences, forgive, and seek reconciliation. We are grateful for the privilege of being part of Your church, and we earnestly pray for the manifestation of unity that brings glory to Your name. Amen.*

DAY 29
SEEKING GOD'S GUIDANCE

**Discover the importance of seeking God's
guidance in decision-making
Read Proverbs 3, focusing on verses 5-6**

Pray for wisdom and discernment in your choices in our 29th devotion, let's delve into the significance of seeking God's guidance when making decisions, a practice essential to our faith journey. This approach aligns our choices with God's divine will, leading to wisdom and inner peace. Let's begin by meditating on Proverbs 3:5-6: "Trust in the LORD with all your heart and lean not on your own understanding; in all your ways submit to him, and he will make your paths straight."

This passage urges us to wholeheartedly trust the Lord and let go of our dependence on human reasoning. It invites us to surrender our decisions to Him, acknowledging His sovereignty and perfect wisdom. When we actively seek God's guidance, we invite Him into every aspect of our lives, recognizing that He knows what is best for us. This practice helps us avoid impulsive or self-centered choices, aligning us with His divine plans.

In the face of various decisions and challenges, it's crucial to pray for wisdom and discernment.

James 1:5 reminds us, "If any of you lack wisdom, you should ask God, who gives generously... and it will be given to you." God is eager to bestow His wisdom, but we must actively seek it through prayer. As we continue our faith journey, let's always remember the importance of seeking God's guidance in our decision-making process. Trust in Him wholeheartedly, pray fervently for wisdom, and willingly surrender our choices to His perfect will. May God abundantly bless you as you seek His guidance in every aspect of your life.

Prayer: *Heavenly Father, today I seek Your divine guidance in my decision-making. I acknowledge You as the source of all wisdom and place my trust in Your knowledge of what is best for me. Help me not to rely on my understanding but on Your leading in every area of my life. Grant me wisdom and discernment as I navigate choices and challenges. Reveal Your will and guide me along the path You have prepared. In Jesus' name, I pray. Amen.*

DAY 30
REFLECTING GOD'S LIGHT

Reflect on your role as a reflection of God's light in the world
Read Matthew 5, focusing on verses 14-16

Pray for the strength to shine God's light in your words and actions as we conclude our 40-day devotion journey, let's reflect on our role as bearers of God's light in the world. In the midst of life's busyness, we often forget our calling to embody His love and grace.

Today, let's meditate on Matthew 5:14-16: "You are the world's light. A city on a hill cannot be hidden. Nor do people light a lamp and put it under a basket. They put it on a lampstand, and it lights up the entire home. Allow your light to shine before others so that they can notice your good acts and worship your heavenly Father." Consider the relevance of the following words: We are the world's light! We cannot hide the light that God has placed inside us, just as a city on a hill cannot be hidden. It is intended to radiate and influence others around us. Consider how you've been expressing God's light through your words and actions. Were there times when fear or doubt dimmed that light? Identify areas for improvement and become more intentional about reflecting His love and grace.

While meditating on this, pray for the strength and courage to shine God's light brightly. Ask Him to daily fill you with His Spirit, empowering you to manifest His love, kindness, and mercy through your words and deeds. Take a moment today to consider how you can intentionally illuminate God's light in your daily life. May His light guide your actions, bringing glory to His name.

Prayer: *Heavenly Father, thank You for appointing me as a beacon of Your light in this world. Help me embrace this calling daily and let Your love and grace radiate through me. Forgive me for the moments when fear or doubt concealed Your light. Strengthen me, Lord, and fill me with Your Spirit, so I can boldly shine Your light in every situation. Grant me the wisdom to recognize opportunities to manifest Your love and goodness in my interactions with others. May my words and deeds glorify You and draw others closer to Your heart. Amen.*

DAY 31
THE SOURCE OF LOVE

Read 1 John 4, focusing on verse 7-8
Dear friends let us love one another for love comes from God.
Everyone who loves has been born of God and knows God.
Whoever does not love does not know God because Gos is love.

Entering the holy season, let us not forget that God is the ultimate origin of love. His love is not temporary or dependent on conditions; it is everlasting and steadfast. This passage urges us to show affection towards each other, emphasizing that our capacity to love comes from our connection with God. The greater our encounter with His love, the better equipped we are to pass it on.

During the hustle and bustle of life, we have a chance to pause and contemplate how we both receive and give love. In the busyness of day-to-day life, we can often overlook the profound love that God has for us. Today, spend some time calming your heart and allowing His love to envelop you. Allow it to refresh your soul and make you more compassionate towards others.

As we travel during this period of 40 days to think and get ready, let's purposefully spread God's love to those around us. Allow His love to flow through you, whether it be in simple acts of kindness or more profound expressions of care. Each act of love mirrors the presence of the divine that resides inside us.

Prayer: *Lord, we are grateful to You for being the origin of all love. Assist me in finding peace in Your love both today and throughout this season of reflection. Help me learn to care for others with the same love and kindness*

You show me. May Your love direct my speech and behavior, leading me nearer to You. So be it.

DAY 32
THE GREATEST OFFERING

Read John 3, focusing on verse 16
God loved the world so much that He gave His only Son, so whoever believes in Him will have eternal life instead of perishing.

Today, we take a moment to contemplate one of the most impactful demonstrations of love throughout history - God's ultimate act of sacrifice. His Son, Jesus Christ, fully displays the extent of His love for us. This one act of love altered the path of eternity, allowing for our redemption and everlasting life in the presence of God. It was an expensive, selfless love that demanded nothing in exchange but gave everything. While we reflect on this passage, let's consider the significance of how it applies to us individually. God's love was not just for the entire world, but specifically for each individual person. Jesus gave up his life because of God's deep, personal affection for you. His love saves us from death and also welcomes us into a new life, characterized by grace, forgiveness, and purpose.

As we pause to consider this sacrifice, change your heart and influence your actions. How does understanding this deep love influence your relationships, decisions, and perspective on life? Allow God's love to change how you see yourself and those around you, leading you to feel thankful and a stronger urge to live according to His teachings.

Prayer: *God, thank you for Your deep love shown through the sacrifice of Jesus for me. I am amazed by this amazing gift. Assist me in dwelling in the brightness of Your love, allowing it to pour into every connection I have. I am forever thankful for Jesus' sacrifice and the everlasting life You provide. In the name of God, Amen.*

DAY 33
AFFECTION AND EMPATHY

Read Colossians 3, focusing on verse 12-14
Therefore, as God's chosen perple, holy and dearly lvoed,
clothe yourselves with compassion, kindness, humility,
gentleness and patience. Bear with each other and forgive
one another if any of you has a grievance against someone.
Forgive as the Lord forgave you. And over all these virtues put
on love, which binds them all together in perfect unity.

As God's chosen, cherished, and holy people, put on compassion, kindness, humility, gentleness, and patience. Be patient and show forgiveness towards each other if anyone has a complaint against another person. Forgive others in the same way that the Lord forgave you. Clothe yourselves with love, which unites all virtues in perfect harmony.

We, as children beloved by God, are tasked with mirroring His character through our behaviors and mindsets. Paul's message in the book of Colossians serves as a reminder that believers must possess traits such as compassion, kindness, humility, gentleness, and patience as they are indispensable, not optional. These virtues are manifestations of the love that God has infused within us. However, the passage goes on to highlight that love is the force that binds all things in complete harmony.

Today, we should reflect on how the love of God motivates us to demonstrate empathy and gentleness towards others, particularly those who have hurt us. Forgiving someone can be a challenging but significant way to show love. Nevertheless, we are urged to forgive as the Lord has forgiven us—totally and without conditions.

Today, make an effort to consider someone in your life who could benefit from your love and forgiveness. This person could be a family member, friend, or even someone you knew in the past. Allow the love of God to fill your heart, enabling you to approach reconciliation with compassion and humility. It is in these moments of grace that we encounter the complete power of God's love actively at work within us.

Prayer: *Dear God, I am grateful for dressing me in Your love and compassion. Assist me in demonstrating equal affection towards others, even when it becomes challenging. Teach me how to forgive others just as You have forgiven me, and lead me towards reconciliation with them. Bind all these virtues in me with Your perfect love. Amen.*

DAY 34
LOVE IN ACTION

Read Matthew 25, focusing on verse 40
"The King will reply, 'Truly I tell you, whatever you did for one of the least of these brothers and sisters of mine, you did for me.'"

Today's verse reminds us that love is not just a feeling or words—it is action. Jesus teaches that when we serve others, especially those in need, we are serving Him. Every act of kindness, no matter how small, becomes an opportunity to demonstrate God's love in a tangible way. Whether it's helping a neighbor, offering a word of encouragement, or volunteering to serve those less fortunate, these acts are sacred in God's eyes.

As we seek to deepen our faith, it invites us to reflect not only on our relationship with God but also on how we live out His love in the world. Are we showing love to those who may be overlooked or marginalized? Do we take the time to serve without expecting anything in return? Love in action has the power to transform not just the lives of others but our own hearts as well.

Today, challenge yourself to go beyond your comfort zone. Find a way to serve someone in need, whether it's giving your time, resources, or simply offering a listening ear. In doing so, you'll experience the joy of encountering God's love through service and seeing His presence in the faces of those you help.

Prayer: *Lord Jesus, thank you for teaching me that serving others is an expression of love for You. Help me to recognize opportunities to serve and to do so with a heart full of compassion and kindness. May every act of service reflect Your love and bring me closer to You. Amen.*

DAY 35
THE COMFORT OF GOD'S LOVE

Read Psalm 139, focusing on verse 7-10
"Where can I go from your Spirit? Where can I flee from your presence? If I go up to the heavens, you are there; if I make my bed in the depths, you are there. If I rise on the wings of the dawn, if I settle on the far side of the sea, even there your hand will guide me, your right hand will hold me fast."

Imagine standing on the shore, watching the waves crash against the rocks. The horizon seems endless, and you feel small in comparison to the vastness of the sea. But in that moment, something deeper stirs inside you—the realization that no matter how far you might go, how isolated you might feel, or how lost you become, God is there. His love, like the endless ocean before you, surrounds you. It reaches into every corner of your life, offering comfort, protection, and peace.

Psalm 139 paints a picture of a God who never leaves our side. Whether we are at the highest peaks of joy or the lowest depths of sorrow, His presence is constant. His love is inescapable—not as something to fear, but as a source of profound comfort. There is nowhere we can go where His hand will not guide us, and His love will not hold us fast.

Today, in the quiet of this journey, allow yourself to rest in that knowledge. Spend time in stillness, letting go of your worries, and letting His presence fill you with peace. God's love is your refuge. It is always with you, holding you even in the most uncertain moments. Take comfort in knowing you are never alone.

Prayer: *Lord, thank you for Your constant presence and unfailing love. No matter where I go or what I face, You are there to guide and comfort me. Fill me with the peace that comes from knowing Your love will never let me go. Help me to rest in Your embrace today. Amen.*

DAY 36
THE COMMAND TO LOVE

Read John 15, focusing on verse 12
"My command is this: Love each other as I have loved you."

Imagine sitting with Jesus and hearing these words spoken directly to you: "Love each other as I have loved you." It's a simple command but profoundly challenging. Jesus is calling us to a love that mirrors His own—selfless, unconditional, and sacrificial. His love was demonstrated through His actions, His sacrifices, and His compassion for all. This is the model for how we are to love others.

Today, take a moment to think about what this kind of love looks like in your everyday life. Reflect on the relationships you have—family, friends, colleagues, and even acquaintances. What does it mean to love them as Jesus loves you? How can you show love that goes beyond just words, reaching into your actions and decisions?

Write down some practical ways you can embody this love. Maybe it's through a kind gesture, a listening ear, or a helping hand. Perhaps it's forgiving someone who's hurt you or reaching out to someone in need. Whatever it is, let it be a reflection of the love Jesus showed—a love that is generous and transformative.

By actively choosing to live out this command, we bring a piece of God's love into the world, making it a bit brighter and more compassionate.

Prayer: *Lord Jesus, Your command to love others as You have loved me feels both simple and profound. Help me to understand the depth of Your love and to express it in my daily life. Show me practical ways to love those around me with a heart like Yours. May my actions reflect Your love and bring others closer to You. Amen.*

DAY 37
THE POWER OF LOVE

Read Romans 8, focusing on verse 38-39
"For I am convinced that neither death nor life, neither angels nor demons, neither the present nor the future, nor any powers, neither height nor depth, nor anything else in all creation, will be able to separate us from the love of God that is in Christ Jesus our Lord."

Imagine a love so powerful that nothing could ever tear it away from you—no circumstance, no fear, no distance. This is the kind of love Paul describes in Romans. It's not a fleeting affection or a temporary feeling, but a steadfast, unshakeable bond that endures through every trial and triumph.

Today, let's take a moment to consider areas of our lives where we might feel disconnected from God's love. Maybe it's through personal struggles, doubts, or feelings of unworthiness. Reflect on how these feelings might create a sense of separation between you and the love of God.

Paul's words remind us that nothing—absolutely nothing—can separate us from God's love. No matter how deep our struggles or how dark our fears, His love is always there, surrounding and upholding us. Take time to surrender these feelings of separation to Him. Allow His love to fill the spaces where you might feel distant or alone.

As we reflect on this powerful truth, let it reassure and comfort you, knowing that God's love is a constant presence, never changing and never fading.

Prayer: *Lord, thank You for Your unbreakable, unchanging love. Even when I feel distant or separated, remind me that nothing can ever separate me from Your love. Help me to surrender my feelings of separation and to rest in the assurance of Your constant presence. Fill my heart with the peace that comes from knowing Your love is always with me. Amen.*

DAY 38
LOVE AND OBEDIENCE

Read John 14, focusing on verse 15
If you love me, you will keep my commandments.

Jesus speaks very clearly in this verse. For Him, love is not simply a feeling or a thought—it is shown through what we do, especially in how we follow His instructions. If we claim to have love for God, that love should result in obedience as a natural outcome. It is love that motivates us to live according to His teachings, not because we have to but because we want to.

Pause for a moment and consider how this manifests in your own personal experiences. Is there any aspect of your behavior that could be more in harmony with God's desires? Perhaps it lies within your relationships, routines, or decisions – places where you feel God is softly urging you to have more faith in Him, to be more devoted, or to release things that are not aligning with His plan for you.

Following instructions can be difficult, especially when it involves giving up power or moving beyond our usual boundaries. However, Jesus does not request obedience to overwhelm us; He urges us to adhere to His commands as they result in life, freedom, and a stronger relationship with Him.

Today, request God's guidance in finding where He wants you to be more in sync with His plan. Ask for the inner fortitude and insight to walk in His ways, understanding that every act of compliance is a gesture of affection that brings you nearer to His love.

Prayer: *Lord, I adore You and desire to walk in Your path. Assist me in demonstrating that love by following commands. Reveal to me the specific* *areas where I must adjust my actions to match Your will, and grant me the courage and insight to follow Your path. Thank You for leading me with kindness and elegance. Amen.*

DAY 39
CULTIVATING A LOVING RELATIONSHIP

Read Jeremiah 31, focusing on verse 3
"I have loved you with a love that never ends; I have attracted you with endless kindness."

Picture listening to these words being spoken straight to your heart: "I have loved you with a love that will never end." It serves as a reminder that God's love for us is everlasting, steadfast, and surpasses our complete understanding. Since our creation, He has been guiding us towards Him, using His kindness and grace to lead us.

As we deepen our relationship with God, we are encouraged to strengthen our connection with Him, the one who has loved us since the start. Relationships develop by investing time, trust, and communicating effectively. Likewise, we cultivate our connection with God through reading His Word, engaging in prayer to seek His presence, and remaining attentive to hear His voice.

Make a conscious effort today to deepen your relationship with God. Whether you choose to read a Scripture passage, write in your journal, or simply sit quietly, allow His eternal love to fill your soul. Consider how His benevolence has helped you overcome life's obstacles and how He consistently brings you nearer to Him. While you invest time in being with Him, believe that this bond will strengthen, similar to how relationships flourish with affection and attention.

Prayer: *Divine Father, I am grateful for Your never-ending love towards me. Assist me in coming nearer to You, in pursuing Your Company, and in hearing Your voice in my everyday life. Help me grow closer to You as I deepen our relationship, and may Your endless love envelop me. So be it.*

DAY 40
LOVE FOR THE WORLD

Read 1 Peter 4, focusing on verse 8
Most importantly, love one another deeply, as love can forgive many wrongdoings.

As we arrive at this stage of our journey, Peter's words highlight the change-inducing strength of love. Love isn't limited to personal connections; it has the power to transform the world. The love that God fills our hearts with should spill over, reaching out to others, particularly those facing difficulties or pain.

We reside in a world frequently torn apart by suffering, rage, and separation. However, Peter urges us to love profoundly, as love can heal, forgive, and reconcile. Choosing to love means we are deciding to mirror God's grace. Our love has the ability to heal wounds, both ours and those of others, because it reflects the forgiveness and compassion of Christ.

When we finish our prayer session, think about ways you can spread God's love in your local area. Search for chances to provide kindness, forgiveness, and support. It could be by performing a small act of kindness, offering a gentle gesture, or showing support to someone facing challenges. When we have a deep love, we bring a small taste of God's kingdom to the world.

Prayer: *Lord, we are grateful for Your endless and persistent love. Assist me in embodying that love in the world. Help me see and understand the needs of people, especially those facing challenges, and grant me the ability to show them love in the same way that You do. May my love provide comfort for wounds and inspire optimism. Amen.*

CONCLUSION

Congratulations on completing this transformative 40-day devotional journey! Your achievement brings me genuine joy. I sincerely hope that the profound experiences you've had with God our ABBA Father during this period will remain a lasting wellspring of inspiration, continually shaping and elevating your faith.

Understanding that your relationship with God is an ongoing odyssey of growth and intimacy is paramount. To nurture this intimacy connection, remain steadfast in your dedication through prayer, diligent study of His Word, nurturing fellowship with fellow believers, and selfless service to those around you. By anchoring yourself deeply in Him, your faith will not only flourish but also usher in His abundant blessings into your life. My heartfelt prayer is that God showers you with boundless blessings as you continue to walk hand in hand with Him, fervently seeking His divine guidance and selflessly sharing His love with the world. May your life shine brightly with His light, and may His grace and peace continually embrace you. Always remember to continue nurturing your faith, knowing that He is steadfastly by your side, guiding every step you take.

Sending you my warmest wishes for continued blessings and profound growth on your remarkable journey with Him!

In His Service,

Karyn Lee

ABOUT THE AUTHOR

A Christ follower who experienced Jesus' love at the age of 11, Karyn Lee came from a small charming tin mining town of Kampar in Perak, West Malaysia. However, her life's trajectory deviated drastically when she was given away at birth. Believing that it was God leading and guiding her, even at a tender age, she came into the care of a compassionate woman who graciously welcomed her into her heart and home. Through her benevolence, Karyn received invaluable gifts, including that of education, a blessing that eventually led her to Singapore in 1976 and later to Australia in 1983, where she completed a business course.

In the intricate fabric of her life, a turning point materialised in 1995 when she encountered a Bible-walking man, who knew the Bible from front to back, embodying his faith. Their subsequent marriage marked the commencement of a shared odyssey. His profession whisked them to various corners of the world, enabling them to immerse themselves in diverse cultures and embrace the essence of international living.

Her journey has brought her back to Australia, where her children are forging their own paths and diligently advancing in their careers. Meanwhile, her husband remains dedicated to his work overseas. Together, they gracefully navigate the delicate balance of a life enriched by diverse experiences and global connections.

www.karyninternational.com

www.ingramcontent.com/pod-product-compliance
Lightning Source LLC
LaVergne TN
LVHW051153080426
835508LV00021B/2598